700030057799

See how plants grow
Leaves

Nicola Edwards

WAYLAND

First published in 2007 by Wayland

Copyright © Wayland 2007

Wayland
338 Euston Road
London NW1 3BH

Wayland Australia
Hachette Children's Books
Level 17/207 Kent Street
Sydney, NSW 2000

British Library Cataloguing in Publication Data

Edwards, Nicola
  Leaves. - (See how plants grow)
  1. Leaves - Juvenile literature
  I. Title
  581.4'8

  ISBN-13: 978-0-7502-5005-4

Editor: Dereen Taylor
Designer: Elaine Wilkinson

Printed in China

Wayland is a division of
Hachette Children's Books.

The publishers would like to thank the following for allowing us to reproduce their pictures in this book:

Alamy: cover (David J King), 22 (Dave King/dk). Corbis: title page and 14 (Phil Schermeister), 5 (Nigel J. Dennis/Gallo Images), 6 (Gavriel Jecan), 7 (Andrianna Williams/zefa), 8 (Dietrich Rose/zefa), 11 (John M Roberts), 12 (Michael Boys), 13 (Micro Discovery), 15 (Gary Braasch), 16 (Tony Craddock/zefa), 18, 20 (Hugh Sitton/zefa), 21 (Dallas & John Heaton/Free Agents Ltd). Ecoscene: 4 (Joel Creed), 19 (Sally Morgan). Getty Images: 17 (Taxi). NHPA: 23 (Stephen Krasemann). Nature Picture Library: 9 (Larry Michael). Science Photo Library: 10 (Steve Taylor).

Contents

What are leaves? 4

What do leaves look like? 6

Leaves in hot and cold areas 8

How do leaves start to grow? 10

What are leaves for? 12

How do leaves make food? 14

How do leaves change? 16

Defence and attack 18

How do we use leaves? 20

Grow your own leaves 22

Glossary 24

Index 24

What are leaves?

Leaves grow on plants, mostly above the ground, although they can grow underwater too. Leaves are important parts of plants. Plants breathe through their leaves and leaves make food for the growing plants.

▼ The huge leaves of the Amazon water lily measure more than two metres across.

Green-leaved plants provide food for people and animals. We eat the leaves themselves or other parts of the plants, such as their **fruit** or **seeds**.

▲ With its thick lips and long tongue, this giraffe can eat the leaves of tall, prickly trees.

What do leaves look like?

Leaves can be huge or tiny, long or short, wide or narrow. They can have smooth or jagged edges, sharp points or rounded ends. Some leaves are sticky or have a waxy surface.

▲ How many different leaf shapes can you see in this area of rainforest?

Leaf Fact

Not all leaves are green. The leaves of the Poinsettia plant, for example, are red.

Tubes called **veins** run through
a leaf. Like the bones in
our bodies these veins
support the leaf.

▲ The veins take
water and **nutrients**
to every part of
the leaf.

Leaves in hot and cold areas

Leaves vary in different parts of the world. Thin, needle-like leaves grow on **conifers** in cold areas.

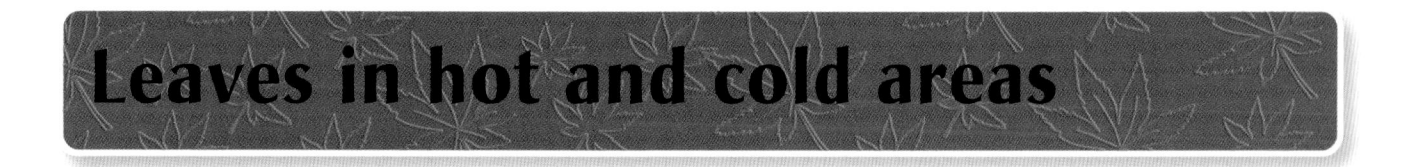

▼ Can you see the needle-like leaves on this conifer?

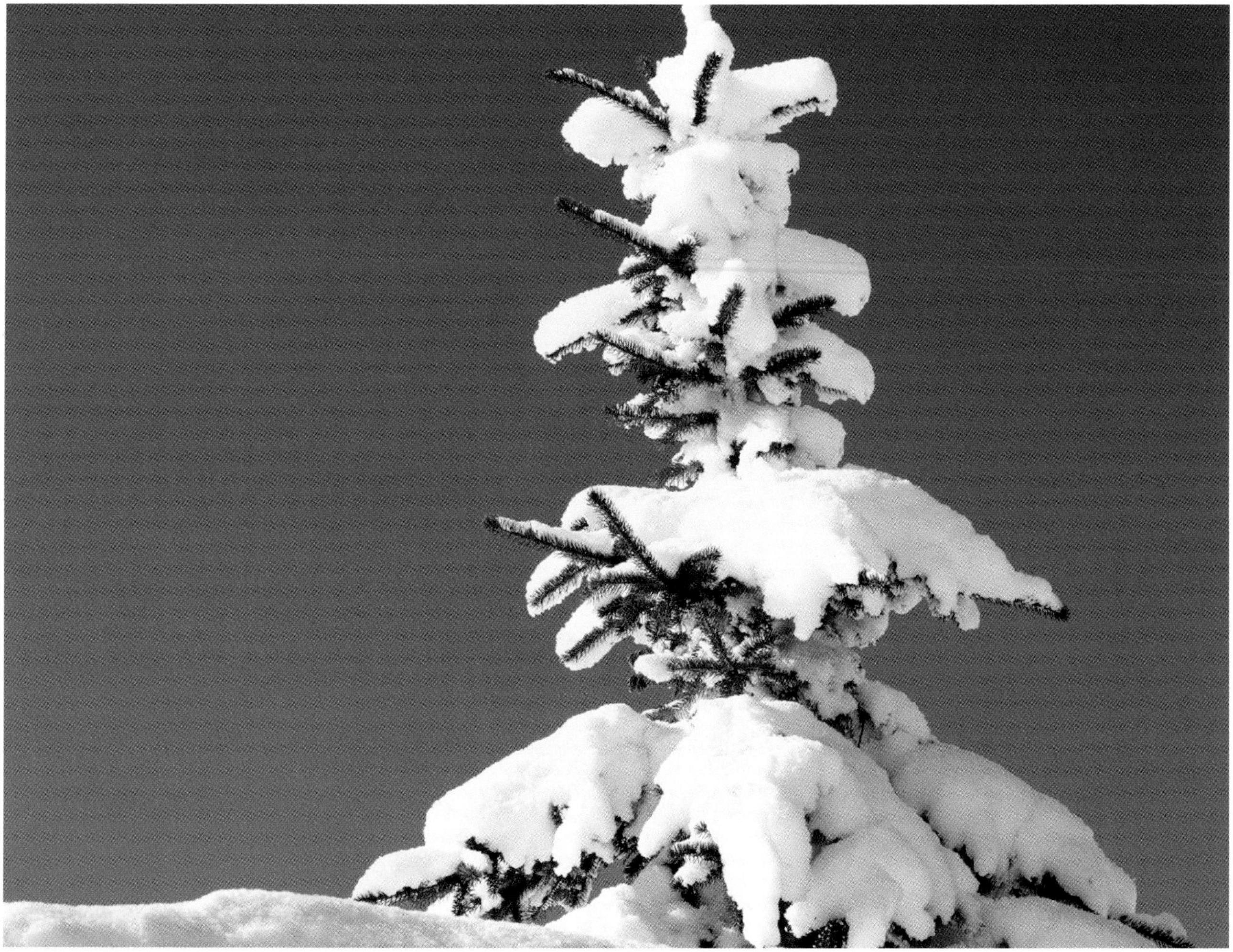

Plants need water to grow. In dry areas leaves are sometimes covered in hairs, spines or scales. This helps to stop the plants from losing too much water.

▲ These prickly spines are the leaves of the cactus plant.

How do leaves start to grow?

When a seed is planted underground, it needs water, warmth and usually soil to grow. The seed **germinates** and begins to grow. A shoot carrying the plant's first leaves pushes upwards from it. These leaves were part of the seed, which contained food to fuel growth.

▼ You can see this sunflower plant's first leaves appearing through the soil.

Leaf Fact

Leaves use water, sunlight and **carbon dioxide** to make food for plants.

▲ As new leaves grow they take over the job of making food for the developing plant.

What are leaves for?

Leaves make food for the growing plant. They allow the plant to breathe and they control the amount of water it contains.

Rhubarb leaves store water for the growing plant.

Leaf Fact

Plants can take in nutrients and gases through their leaves even if they are growing underwater.

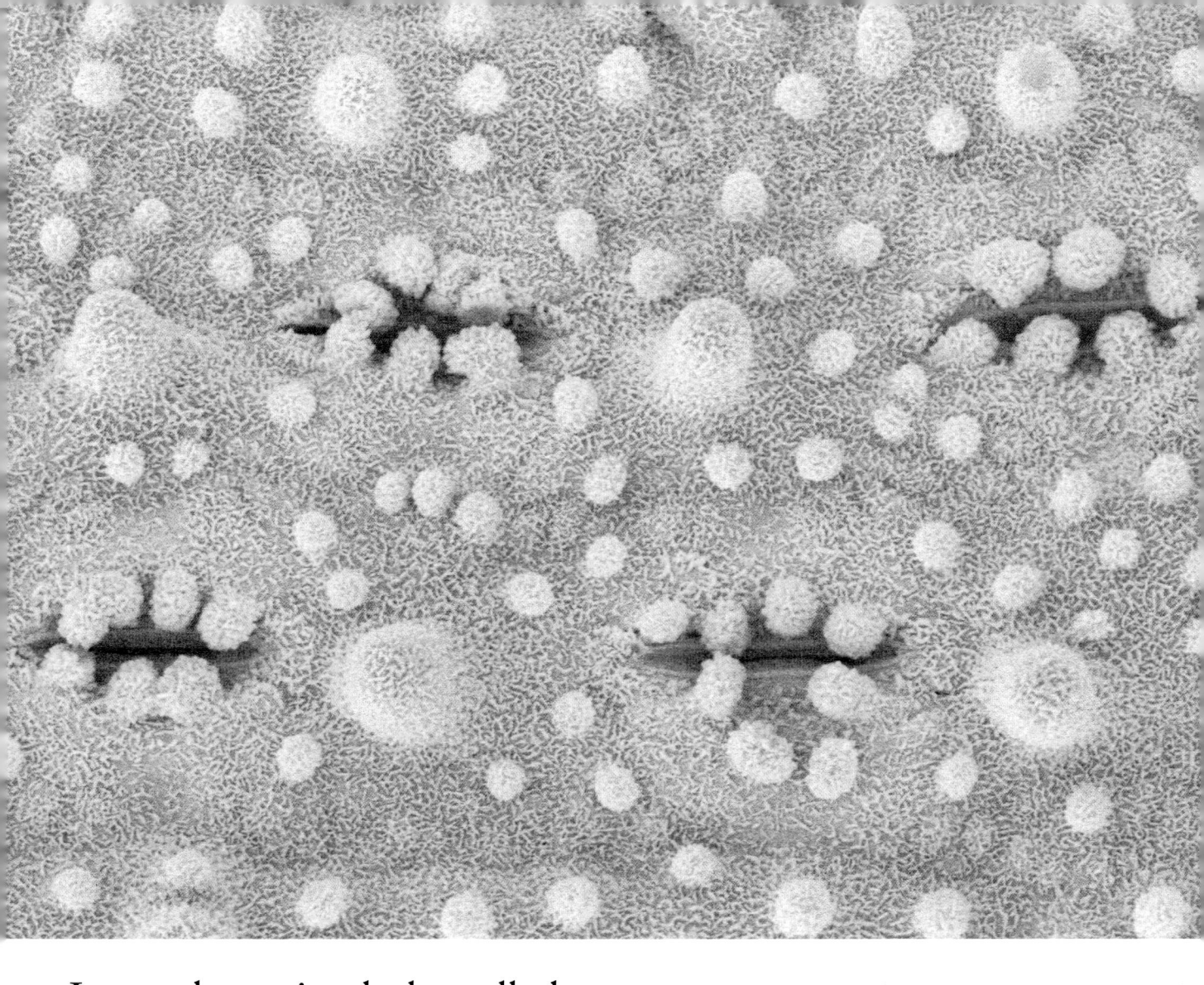

Leaves have tiny holes called **stomata** on their undersides. These holes can open and close to allow gases - carbon dioxide, **oxygen** and **water vapour** - to pass in and out of the leaf.

▲ In this picture, the stomata have been magnified many times so that you can see them clearly.

How do leaves make food?

Leaves contain **chlorophyll**. This gives them their green colour and helps them to make food. The leaves use energy from sunlight. This energy turns water from the soil and carbon dioxide from the air into food for the plant.

▼ The chlorophyll in leaves helps them to make food.

When leaves make food they produce a gas called oxygen. We need to breathe oxygen to live.

These fern leaves, called fronds, grow in a pattern to make sure that each leaf receives as much sunlight as possible.

How do leaves change?

The leaves of **broadleaved trees** change in the autumn as the days become colder. Their colour changes from green to gold, red and brown. The leaves fall from the branches and the trees remain bare throughout the winter. In spring, as the days become warmer, leaf buds grow on the branches.

▲ Leaf buds start to open to reveal new leaves.

Leaf Fact

In autumn the chlorophyll fades from the leaves, allowing other colours to show through.

▼ How many colours can you see in these leaves?

Defence and attack

Some leaves have ways to stop animals eating them. They may have prickly edges, like holly, or stinging hairs, like nettles.

The sharp, spiky edges of these holly leaves stop hungry animals from coming too close!

Some leaves, such as thyme, contain strong smelling oils which make animals avoid them. The leaves of meat-eating plants can trap their prey.

▲ The hinged leaves of this Venus flytrap snap shut, trapping insects inside them.

How do we use leaves?

We can eat leaves such as spinach and cabbage raw or cooked. We use the fresh and dried leaves of scented herbs like mint to add flavour to food. Leaves are used to make medicines, too. The dried leaves of the coconut palm are woven or plaited and made into baskets and mats.

▼ The dye used to make these decorative patterns comes from the crushed leaves of the henna plant.

These leaves are used to make tea, one of the world's favourite drinks.

Grow your own leaves

You can grow all sorts of leafy plants from seeds. You could grow cress, basil or dill and then taste the leaves.

Fill a pot with soil and sprinkle a few seeds on top. Then cover the seeds with soil.

▲ You could also try soaking bean seeds in water and then plant them. The tiny leaves inside each seed will begin to grow.

Leaf Fact

Some leaves are poisonous. Don't touch any leaves until you are sure they are safe.

Water the soil gently and keep it damp. Put the pot in a warm place and watch your plant grow.

Can you see the roots of this bean seedling?

Glossary

broadleaved trees
Trees that have wide, flat leaves and produce flowers and fruit.

carbon dioxide
A gas in air that leaves use to make food.

chlorophyll
The substance that gives leaves their green colour and helps them to make food.

conifers
Trees with thin, spiny leaves. Conifers produce cones.

fruit
The part of a plant that contains seeds.

germinate
When a seed starts to develop into a plant.

nutrients
Food in the soil that a plant needs for growth.

oxygen
A gas that leaves produce when they make food. People need to breathe oxygen to live.

seeds
The parts of a plant from which new plants develop.

stomata
Holes in the underside of a leaf through which gases pass in and out.

veins
Tubes in a leaf that carry water and nutrients to every part of it.

water vapour
Water in the form of a gas.

Index

broadleaved trees 16

cacti 9

carbon dioxide 10, 13, 14

chlorophyll 14, 16

conifers 8

dried leaves 20

eating leaves
    animals 5, 18-19

humans 5, 20

fruit 5

germination 10

growing leafy plants 22-23

insects 19

leaf buds 16

leaves
    as medicines 20
    changing colour 16-17

making their food 4,10-11,12,14-15
    under water 4, 12

nutrients 7, 12

oxygen 13, 15

poisonous leaves 22

scented leaves 19, 20

seeds 5, 10, 22

stomata 13

sunlight 10, 14, 15

veins 7

water
    importance of 9, 10, 14
    intake 7, 12

water vapour 13